Managing Relationships at Work

Building Effective & Healthy Working Relationships

Gerard Assey

Contents

Preface

Building positive workplace relationships is vital for career and organizational success. Relationships can affect the satisfaction on the job, as well as one's ability to advance and gain recognition for the achievements. According to Gallup Organization, the top American analytics and advisory company, people who have a best friend at work are seven times more likely to be engaged in their jobs. And it doesn't have to be a best friend: Gallup found that people who simply had a good friend in the workplace are more likely to be satisfied.

We all work with others in our daily working life to produce the products and services that we provide to our customers. It is important to maintain happy relationships with all those people we work with to ensure that our work gets done efficiently, so that our customers receive the right type of service they require.

Much of what managers and supervisors accomplish is done through their leadership and support of others. Healthy relationships are therefore central to this process. However, all too often, responding to short-term task pressures keeps us from making long-term investments in strong relationships. To be successful as a manager or supervisor we need to develop strong relationship building skills. Healthy relationships require a level of interpersonal interaction, trust, and rapport that is also required to sustain relationships in our personal lives. From that standpoint, we use the same competencies and skill sets for building healthy relationships in all facets of our lives. Therefore building effective workplace relationships is an extremely important skill for every employee. The strength of our relationship building skills can affect our ability to negotiate effectively, deliver products and projects, meet deadlines and make progress in our career.

This little, but powerful guide will therefore help provide the necessary components of healthy relationships as a way to understanding and leveraging on the relationships you have in your organization. Various strategies are provided as tools for working with and through others. When you build positive relationships, you feel more comfortable with your interactions and less intimidated by others. You feel a closer bond with the people you spend the majority of your time working with. For a lot of people, relationship building isn't natural or easy to do. Most refuse to admit this is a concern because it is a basic common-sense concept, and they assume they already know how to do it. However, everyone, even the most outgoing engaging personalities, can improve their skills in this critical area. Your ability to create and maintain healthy and productive relationships with people at all levels of the organization is an important factor in your ultimate effectiveness as a leader.

It's interesting to note that human beings working in an office are very much like a box of crayons- all different in nature, culture, size, color, education, experience etc., but all fitted well in one box (the organization) each having a different role like a crayon to play when required. And when used together, with healthy relationships the picture is complete and beautiful-A masterpiece!

Objectives of this Book: What will this Book help you Achieve?

You will be able to:
- ✓ Build and maintain healthy relationships in your work environment.
- ✓ Apply the techniques and skills that promote good and healthy team relations.
- ✓ Effectively get work done through others.
- ✓ Effectively handle conflict and treat each other with mutual respect and goodwill.
- ✓ Increase productivity and work satisfaction.
- ✓ Achieve moral support and assistance with meeting difficult timelines.
- ✓ Develop and manage peer-to-peer relationships and your "social network."
- ✓ Communicate more effectively with staff, superiors, customers and vendors.
- ✓ Overall, help Improve in your personal growth

Exercise

List the various objectives you have in mind (for you/ your organization/ others) by you reading this book?

1.
2.
3.
4.
5.
6.
7.
8.

Importance of Developing Good Relationships at Work: Why have Good Relationships at Work?

Ethologists and Zoologists can tell us of what exactly happens in the animal kingdom. When observing the natural behavior in the animal kingdom, there are clear signs of rules of behavior between one another. The young monkey does not mess around with the other bigger animals and when lions are feeding on a freshly killed carcass the hyenas know very well that they better keep a good distance. And, nobody has taught them any of this. All of this behavior seems to be instinctual or intuitive but it gives a very clear purpose and message of maintaining order within a kingdom. So how much more with us, the human beings- considered with super intelligence! And yet, sadly, this is most times the very reason for chaos in organizations and even with some nations. Human beings are naturally social creatures- we crave for friendship and positive interactions, just as we do for food and water. So it makes sense that the better our relationships are at work, the happier and more productive we're going to be.

It is interesting to see what came about from a recent study conducted on the top 500 CEO's worldwide. The survey asked each of these top 500 CEO's the following question: *"If you are to retire or to step down and if you had to look for a person to take your place, what are some of the traits that you would look for in the new CEO?"* Well, several different traits came about in that list, but I want to share just the top 3. Any guesses as to what they could be?

Right on to top of the list as number 1, was 'integrity'. And this should not come as a surprise, as if this ingredient is missing in the top man, you could imagine the state of the rest in the organization. What followed as number 2 was 'communication and presentation skills', with 'Inter-personal skills & Relationship Building' (the ability to get along with others, in a team, or as a team leader etc) ranking as number 3.

Most certainly, as can be seen again, this is one of the most essential skills, especially as you keep moving up the ladder. The higher you go up, the more crucial this skill becomes.

Good working relationships give us several benefits- to the individual as well as the organization:

- ✓ People help people they know, like and trust and when you help others, they will help you
- ✓ When co-workers help each other, the company moves forward
- ✓ Our work is more enjoyable when we have good relationships with those around us
- ✓ People are more likely to go along with changes that we want to implement
- ✓ We tend to be more innovative and creative with the cooperation of others
- ✓ Healthy relationships make us happier, motivated and more productive
- ✓ A strong network can help with career advancement
- ✓ Good relationships give us freedom: instead of spending time and energy overcoming the problems associated with negative relationships, we can, instead, focus on opportunities.

- ✓ Good relationships are very much necessary if we are to develop our careers. After all, if your boss doesn't trust you, it's unlikely that he or she will consider you when a new position opens up.
- ✓ Will be able to handle conflict effectively and treat each other with mutual respect and goodwill, thus improving morale in the workplace.
- ✓ Overall, we all want to work with people we're on good terms with as it gives us the peace of mind and a good night's sleep.
- ✓ We also need good working relationships with others in our professional circle- Customers, suppliers and key stakeholders are all essential to our success. So, it's important to build and maintain good relations with these people
- ✓ Helps with improved personal growth and development, as we don't need to spend much time handling interpersonal office challenges and politics- can focus on professional development.
- ✓ Increased satisfaction with our careers
- ✓ Increased comfort with presentations and team meetings
- ✓ Moral support and assistance with meeting difficult timelines
- ✓ Lesser attrition for the organization
- ✓ Having good working relationships with senior staff also means that we can benefit from their knowledge and learn from mentors.

Exercise

What are some of the Key Benefits to you as an Individual, as well as to your organization by building on Good Working Relationships?

You:

1.
2.
3.
4.
5.
6.
7.
8.

Organization:

1.
2.
3.
4.
5.
6.
7.
8.

What is a Good Relationship?
Defining a Good Relationship

Working relationships are the connections we form with coworkers, colleagues and managers in the workplace. Although the relationships we build with colleagues and managers may not be as intimate as those we have with family and friends, they are nonetheless crucial. Healthy relationships involve honesty, trust, respect and open communication between one another and they take effort, understanding and compromise from both sides.

There are several characteristics that make up good, healthy working relationships:

- ✓ Trust- This is the foundation of every good relationship. When you trust your team and colleagues, you form a powerful bond that helps you to work and communicate more effectively. If you trust the people you work with, you can be open and honest in your thoughts and actions, and you don't have to waste time and energy trying to see what is happening behind your back- who is trying to stab you from behind.
- ✓ Mutual Respect- When you respect the people who you work with, you value their inputs, suggestions and ideas, and they value yours. By working together, you can develop solutions based on these collective insights, wisdom and creativity.
- ✓ Self-awareness- By taking responsibility for your words and actions, and not letting your own negative emotions impact the people around you.
- ✓ Welcoming Diversity- People with good relationships not only accept diverse people and opinions, but they welcome them. They are able to blend well instantly.
- ✓ Open Communication- We communicate all day, whether we're sending emails, on phone or meeting face to face. The better and more effectively we communicate with those around us, the richer our relationships will be. All good relationships depend on open, transparent and honest communication

Exercise

What according to you are some other characteristics that make up good, healthy relationships?

1.
2.
3.
4.
5.

Types of Work Relationships

The Workplace is where we spend roughly one third of our lives and, in the process, where we encounter a variety of people. Although dealing with workplace relationships of all kinds can be difficult, it can also bring a sense of togetherness and genuine friendship and therefore workplace relationship ethics are imperative to having successful business partnerships with the people you encounter during an entire week- but those very same relationships can be tricky to navigate. Learning how to navigate workplace relationships can help to build your network and boost your reputation as a professional

Here are some of the type of Relationships you would need to work with:

Office friends: A work friend is someone you interact with in a more casual, social way. More than likely, these are people you collaborate with regularly or who share your workspace or work within physical proximity of you. Your work friends are often coworkers or team members you interact with at the office. These interactions may also extend to professional events or casual events outside of the office. You know enough about each others' lives to have some jokes, and they're a reliable shoulder to lean on. Your work friends serve as part of your support system, and maintaining these relationships is usually mutually beneficial.

Colleagues: This is purely professional. A colleague is the person on your team that you say hello to but don't go past basic chit chat or work-related conversations. They could be from other departments and usually on the same level and pay scale as you and they're ultimately the people you actually need to work well with in order to accomplish your tasks. These people work closely with you, usually on a specific project. Together, you plan, develop and execute work that makes a big difference in your company. These relationships usually remain professional.

Manager/ Boss: This relationship is entirely professional and circumstantial. In most cases, there is little daily interaction, except for the professional meetings or briefings with your direct report beyond morning greetings as you'd typically be working more frequently alongside your fellow colleagues in similar roles. The manager assigns you the work and leads the team. This is a vital relationship, helping you grow in the company. They determine whether you receive a pay rise, promotion and restructure things like your hours or tasks.

Mentor/ Mentee: Typically, a mentor is sought out by a new hire or even a longtime employee looking to move up the ladder and leverage their talents with a little guidance from a seasoned professional. As a mentor, your advice and feedback should be timely, accurate and based on personal or professional experience. The mentor strikes the balance between professional and personal relationship. It's a more intimate version of a leader or manager, guiding you through the work landscape to help you succeed. While it's usually a one-on-one, the basis of your relationship is work.

Mentee – seeks guidance and advice from experienced professionals who have traveled your path. A mentee is an official or unofficial professional learner. If you support a mentee, your role is advisory and interactive. Your mentee is likely to come to you with questions about gaining skills, developing professional relationships and subject area expertise. Mentor-to-mentee relationships should be professional, sympathetic and communicative.

Client/ Supplier: A client/ supplier relationship is one between you and a client or vendor of the business or organization. Most for-profit companies maintain relationships with the customers they provide goods or services for. Depending on your role, you may interact with Individual customers, vendors, suppliers or people who represent departments within a client company.

Subordinates: If you hold a leadership position, you are likely to maintain relationships with people who report to you. Whether you are a team leader, supervisor, c-suite member or manager, the parameters of this relationship should be friendly, impartial, goal-oriented and communicative. Clear boundaries should be set to distinguish this supervisory relationship from other types of colleague or coworker relationships.

As can be seen from above, there are various types of relationships one will need to adjust with and move along if one has to be successful. However, most times, it would be these four types that will surround you- like a sandwich as in the illustration below:

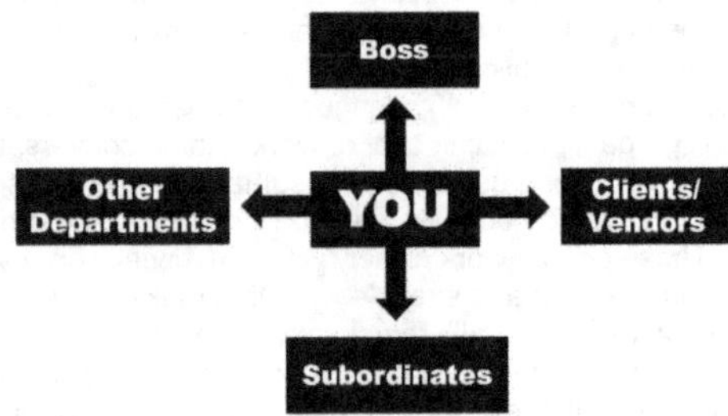

Where and with Whom to Build Good Relationships

Although we should try to build and maintain good working relationships with everyone, there are certain relationships that deserve extra attention. Here are some thoughts that can help you make a start:

A Mentor: A mentor is someone experienced, who has gone through the mill already and will help you navigate through life with you going through the 'school of hard knocks'. When a more experienced person teaches someone new, the knowledge transfer that takes place is unparalleled. Some of the most successful people have had mentors that have helped catapult their careers upwards on a fast track.

Key Stake Holders/ Sponsor: You'll likely benefit from developing good relationships with key stakeholders in your organization. These are the people who have a stake in your success or failure. Forming a bond with these people will help you to ensure that your projects and career stay on track. Once you've created a list of colleagues who have an interest in your projects and career, you can devote time to building and managing these relationships. You could begin by showing people in your organization that you're someone worth advocating for. This means you must be great at what you do and your work must be visible, by keeping your word and commitments

Clients/ Customers/ Suppliers: These are another group that deserve extra attention. Good relationships with your clients/ customers/suppliers can lead to extra sales, career advancement, and a more rewarding life

Competition: Your relationship with your competitor is equally important: When used correctly and in a healthy manner, it can serve as a motivation to hone and improve your skills and lead to improved performance, breakthrough ideas, and a greater drive to get things done.

Exercise

Who are the ones you would specifically like to build strong relationships with? List!

1.
2.
3.
4.
5.
6.
7.
8.

Factors Affecting and Influencing Relationships

What factors Affect and Influence Relationships?
We are all individuals and respond differently to various types of situations and other people.
We may find that we get along better with certain people in the organization than others and it may be due to many factors

So what are those factors that affect and influence one's relationships?
- ✓ Age
- ✓ Social background
- ✓ Same taste in music, sport, hobbies
- ✓ Same sense of humor
- ✓ Common job role
- ✓ Sometimes the same challenges or problems

Sometimes it can also be influenced by:
- ✓ Organizational structure (management and staff)
- ✓ Personality types (outgoing/quiet)
- ✓ Length of time you spend with people

Exercise
What are some of the other factors that affect and influence relationships? List!
1.
2.
3.
4.
5.
6.
7.
8.

5 Unhealthy Patterns of a Team

Organizations fail to achieve teamwork because they unknowingly fall prey to 5 natural but dangerous pitfalls.
- ✓ Team members who are not genuinely open with one another make it impossible to build a Foundation for Trust
- ✓ Failure to build trust sets the tone for Fear of Conflict.
- ✓ A lack of healthy conflict creates Lack of Commitment.
- ✓ Because of lack of real commitment and buy-in, team members develop an Avoidance of Accountability
- ✓ Failure to hold one another accountable creates an environment of Inattention to Results

This occurs when individual needs (such as ego, career development, own needs, or recognition) are placed above the collective goals of the team.

On the other hand truly Cohesive Teams…
- ✓ Trust one another.
- ✓ Know one another's unique strengths and weaknesses.
- ✓ Openly engage in constructive ideological conflict. Engage in unfiltered conflict around ideas.
- ✓ Hold one another accountable for behaviors and actions.
- ✓ Commit to group decisions and plans of action.
- ✓ Hold one another accountable for delivering against those plans.
- ✓ Focus on the achievement of collective results

Exercise
What according to you (what you've seen/ heard/ experienced) are the key reasons for the downfall of teams?
1.
2.
3.
4.
5.

Exercise
What according to you (what you've seen/ heard/ experienced) are the key reasons for teams bonding together?
1.
2.
3.
4.
5.

The 4 Key Components of Healthy Relationships

There are 4 Key Components of Healthy Relationships- they are easily remembered as the 4C's:

Conditions: Creating a supportive environment in which the relationship can thrive (awareness, authenticity, respect, forgiveness, understanding and trust).

Connection: Working together in ways that improve each person and the ongoing relationship. The goal is for each person to contribute to the relationship and grow from the experience (engagement, empathy, mutuality, vitality and empowerment). For best results, colleagues and business partners need to feel connected, working towards a shared goal. This level of understanding encourages trust and openness, and nurtures acceptance and shared values. Connection takes time to develop, and not everyone realizes its importance. But you can build it through constant feedback, involving openness and appreciation.

Commitment: The same as with personal relationships, commitment means making a mindful and consistent decision to invest in a working relationship. In business, both sides need to work towards its growth. Some people don't need reminding about the need to do this, or how to go about it. But we can all do better.

Communication: Even if you've made a connection and you're committed to your plan, everyday business pressures can lead to communication problems. Talking openly to address and achieve what is important to the relationship and the individuals involved (candor, listening, inquiry and closure)

Let's look deeper into the 1ˢᵗ C- Creating & Sustaining CONDITIONS for Healthy Relationships

Healthy relationships don't just appear or survive on their own. Therefore, managers and supervisors must begin by creating and sustaining the conditions necessary for them to thrive. And there are five conditions that are listed below:

- ✓ Awareness – Both people are aware of how the relationship is doing, based on observations and experiences.
- ✓ Authenticity –If both people are being themselves, less time is spent pretending, and more time is spent attending to what is needed.
- ✓ Respect – Honor and value each person, and appreciate any differences.
- ✓ Flexibility – Create an environment in which there is room for people to make mistakes. No Blame/No Shame.
- ✓ Trust –Trust is the backbone

The 2ⁿᵈ C- The quality of the CONNECTION: How do they relate to each other?

The second component of healthy and productive relationships is the quality of the connection between the parties involved. How do the people relate to each other and what results from how they do so? Below are the key characteristics of healthy connection

- ✓ Engagement – Participation with integrity.
- ✓ Empathy – Stepping outside their views to see the world from another person's perspective.

✓ Mutuality – Being in balance with one another. Even in hierarchies it is important to recognize that learning and enrichment can occur in both directions.
✓ Vitality – A healthy relationship increases your energy and sense of being alive.
✓ Empowerment – Dedication to mutuality in the relationship. More is possible because of the relationship than without it.

How can we evaluate the quality of these Relationships?
If any one of these components is not present to a great degree, you need to consider how you will work to improve the relationship.
1) How engaged am I with the other person in this relationship?
2) How willing am I to stand in this person's shoes with empathy right now?
3) How much respect am I showing this person in this encounter?
4) How much am I in reciprocity and mutuality with this person?
5) How willing am I to increase their power as well as mine in this situation?

3rd C-Commitment of every member in the Team
Just like a footballer who lets his team down by not showing up for matches, people who lack commitment at work can have a negative impact on their team's morale and performance. For this, every member must be willing to put in the time and effort needed if they want to achieve the organization's strategic priorities, by making sure to always keep their eyes on the prize. This will drive commitment in their personal efforts and set the right tone for building cultures of excellence for the people and organizations.
Here are some things that can help:
Team members feel Valued: When team members feel that their work is making a valuable contribution to the organization they will be more committed.
Purpose: Great teams have complete buy-in with their goals and objectives. They may go through a storming stage and can become disagreeable, but more often than not, this leads to better understanding and compromising on the best way of getting something done.
Alignment of Goals: Aligning team goals to company-wide goals is critical to demonstrate how each team's efforts contribute to the organization's success. Teams with goals that are not organizationally aligned often lose their sense of purpose over time. Likewise, when individuals' goals are aligned with their group's goals, team performance improves.
Clarity around Roles and Responsibilities: Ideally, each ones roles and responsibilities should be around their respective strengths and interests.
The Team is stretched: Team members are challenged enough and that they aren't bored. Those who are excited about projects they are working on at work will be more committed to their team and to the company.
Transparency and Openness: Leaders should ensure that their team's goals are visible and have been communicated to relevant parts of the organization. There is enough transparency that exists between top and lower level with opportunity to participate and contribute in various activities.
Give Praise where Praise is due: Praise leads to confidence and renewed energy, and can give team members the final push they need when faced with a difficult task.

Give people permission to fail: it's ok to fail and encourage team members to speak up if they spot any potential issues.

The 4th C- How people COMMUNICATE with each other
The fourth component of healthy relationships is how people communicate with each other. People in healthy relationships are able to have powerful conversations about things that matter to them, even when doing so is difficult.
Below are the characteristics of good communication:
Candor -Get the essential issues on the table and address them with honesty, clarity and respect. Say what you are thinking in ways that promote the conditions for a healthy relationship.
Listening- Take the time to truly hear the other person and their message with depth and respect.
Spaciousness- Make room for each person to express themselves
Enquiring- The other side of listening: being curious and seeking truth. Ask the right type of questions. Help others pursue their own answers.
Reconfirm- Make sure that both people are clear about what has been discussed and agreed to in a conversation

Communication is one of the main KEYS to Healthy Relationships.
Here are some other things that you can keep in mind to work on this area:
- ✓ Acknowledge/greet people with a smile
- ✓ Use polite gestures
- ✓ Maintain eye contact, as appropriate
- ✓ Maintain correct (upright, alert) posture
- ✓ Genuinely show interest in what others are saying
- ✓ Listen more, talk less
- ✓ Ask appropriate Questions-Open & Closed (More on this in the next chapter)

Exercise
Can you identify these 4 components of healthy relationships in your current work relationship experiences? Where do the various aspects of these components come naturally to you in your work relationships? What areas require more work?

Asking the Right Questions and Listening are the KEYS!

Learning to ask better questions in our everyday conversations has enormous benefits on relationships. Firstly, asking appreciative questions improves one's emotional intelligence and demonstrates empathy to the receiver of your question. Also, asking well-considered questions expands the possibilities in the answer and has the potential to deepen a relationship.
However, sadly, we are biased towards telling instead of asking, because we live in a pragmatic, problem-solving culture in which knowing things and telling others what we know is valued .In order to build relationships based on dialogue and mutual respect, it is essential to learn to ask more questions. This shows care and concern.

Questions are a powerful tool to nurture relationships and make them effective and satisfactory for both sides.
If we start asking more questions we will immediately notice the benefits in our relationships with others:
- ✓ We'll understand the **people** we are relating to
- ✓ We'll focus on them and encourage **empathy**
- ✓ We'll allow them to express themselves and give us the **information** we want
- ✓ We'll stimulate their **attention** and their involvement
- ✓ It would indicate that we care and are genuinely concerned.

In order that the communicative exchange is effective and that the dialogue is fluid, it is important to ask the right question, and in order to ask our questions in an effective way, we should ask ourselves "*What do I want to obtain? What do I really need to know?*" this way the exchange of information can go straight to the point
So the art of asking the right questions requires the use of different types of questions. First let us have an understanding of the different types of questions that we could ask someone. Though there are several types of questions, for the purpose of this exercise let us look at just the 3 most important ones ie;
OPEN Questions
CLOSED Questions
FOLLOW-UP Questions
Depending on what type of answer you want from the other person, either of these questions are used.
Eg; If I asked you: *'Did you have your dinner'?*
Or *'Do you like this training session?'* or *'Are you going home this evening'?*
The only possible answer that you could give me would either be a *'yes'* or a *'no'*
That is why this type of question is called a 'closed question', because the only possible answer would be a one word- with either a *'yes'* or *'no'*
Closed questions usually begin with:
'Are you…'
'Will you…'
'Do you…'
'Would you…'

They are usually not very helpful in starting a conversation and extracting information. However, most people are more comfortable asking such questions.

The opposite of 'closed' is the obvious: 'open'. Open questions allow the other person to open up or do the talking and are used to encourage the other side to speak freely about a concern or expand on something already raised during the conversation. Always remember this: Open questions generally begin with 5W's and 1 H ie;

Who?
What?
When?
Where?
Why?
How?

And they encourage the other person to open up and speak.

If we were to redo that example again using open questions, they would go something like this: *'What did you have for dinner?' 'How do you feel about this training?' 'What plans do you have for this evening'?*

These questions will certainly not fetch you a *'yes'* or *'no'* like how closed questions do. But they would allow the other person to open up with information which is what we could be looking forward to, by asking such questions.

Shooting out these questions without any logical order would also be inappropriate, as it could be unprofessional, could be irritating at times and most of all cause confusion in the mind of the other person. But if the other person was taken through a logical pattern, it could help lead him or open up to making the conversation two-way and interesting for both parties

Effective listening involves the use of follow-up questions and they are useful in several ways:

- They show we are interested and encourage the other person to keep talking.
- They increase the quality of the information gained.
- They help us to confirm our understanding of what has been said.

Before we can ask a follow-up question we need to listen to what the other side has said and wait for an appropriate pause in the conversation to ask the question.

Follow-up questions can also take the form of a question asked in response to a statement by the other side. They can reflect the information in the original question by beginning with phrases like:

So you are saying that...?
Does that mean...?
If I understand correctly are you saying that...?

Followed by a summary of what was said by the customer.

Let us see some examples now!
Examples of Open questions:
What exactly do you see the issue as Tim?
How can I help you solve this problem?

These Questions can help to dig into or search for details and are also called Probing Questions:
"Exactly how did this happen?"
"What steps did you take?"

Exercise:
Now write three examples of your own
1.
2.
3.

Examples of Closed questions:
Did you receive the letter we sent you on Friday?
Are you happy with the service you have received?

Exercise:
Now write three examples of your own
1.
2.
3.

Examples of Follow up questions:
What were you told when you rang us?
How quickly were you promised a reply?
In these examples the follow-up questions have been asked in response to the customer saying that he
1) Rang us previously,
2) Was told he would be given a reply

Exercise:
Now write three examples of your own
1.
2.
3.

Exercise:
List at least 5 Open Questions you will ask your subordinate to diagnose the Problem/ begin a conversation!
1.
2.
3.
4.
5.

Listening Skills
Now while the other person talks, you would need to listen attentively.

'People were designed with two ears and one mouth, and that is the ratio in which to use them'!

How to be a good listener?
One of the greatest skills that one can develop is the skill of listening. The best professionals are the ones that do less talking and more of listening and that is why I believe God gave us two ears and one mouth- so we would do more listening than talking!

Listen Actively
- ✓ Focus on the speaker
- ✓ Keep an open mind
- ✓ Tolerate silence
- ✓ Ask open-ended questions
- ✓ Repeat the speaker's thoughts
- ✓ Listen for facts and key words

To be an "active" listener:
- ✓ Suspend judgment, initially
- ✓ Avoid distractions; when on the telephone don't carry on side conversations; when face-to-face make eye contact
- ✓ Assess what you heard
- ✓ Clarify and confirm
- ✓ Take notes of key points
- ✓ Never use your phone in the customer's premises! It's a big disturbance and bad manners!

Before you respond, assess the information you heard by asking yourself four questions:
- ✓ What has he/she told me?
- ✓ What can I do with this information?
- ✓ What else do I need to know?
- ✓ What questions do I still need to ask?

To show you're listening actively:
- ✓ Use terms like, 'Go on', Uh huh' and 'mmm'
- ✓ Stay tuned in/Watch for non-verbal cues

To show that you have, understood:
- ✓ Use, phrases like "I see," "I understand"
- ✓ Paraphrase, "So you want me to …"

Clarifying what they said:
In order to more fully understand what is being said we can make it clearer by asking for more detail:
- ✓ *You said that you were not satisfied with our service...Can you tell me why?*

✓ You mentioned how helpful we had been. Can you elaborate specifically In what way?
✓ You said there had been problems in the past. What were they like?

Exercise:
Now think of three examples of clarifying statements you might make yourself
1.
2.
3.

Exercise

What are areas that you would need to work on to improve your listening skills beginning immediately?

1.

2.

3.

4.

5.

Clarifying and Reconfirming with Closed Questions

This is the time when closed questions are very useful. To clarify and reconfirm, restate in your own words what the other person has said and ask him/her to verify your understanding. An example would be: *'Mr Customer, Let me just take a minute to summarize, just to ensure that I've got the right information…You were mentioning that you were having a problem with….Am I right Mr. So & So?"*

After the other person has confirmed your understanding, you have earned the right to proceed with additional questions to gain more information about the situation.

Why summarize regularly?

- *It keeps complexities under control*
- *It tests progress*
- *It lets you restate what the other party has said*
- *It can help gain the initiative*
- *It can keep the discussion on track*
- *It can prevent misinterpretation, misunderstanding and subsequent bitterness*
- *In other words, summarizing helps you stay on top (but you take the point).*

By summarizing, you are making sure you have the right information and that you haven't left out anything.

Trust, Respect and Understanding-The 3 Key Pillars

Building Trust and the Measures of Trust
Robust communication is an essential part of trust in relationships.
Trust is the backbone for relationships. Without it, not much gets done well.

How to Build Trust?
The first job is to inspire trust. Trust is confidence born of 3 dimensions:
Character, Credibility and Competence
Character includes your integrity, motive, and intent with people.
Competence includes your capabilities, skills, abilities, results, and track record. Both dimensions are vital.
The foundation of trust is your own Credibility, and it can be a real differentiator. When a leader's credibility and reputation are high, it enables them to establish trust fast - speed goes up, cost goes down.

5 Common Measures of Trust
- ✓ Reliability: I trust that if I give this assignment to Rani, she will get it done on time.
- ✓ Candor: I trust that if I ask Raja for his feedback on my proposal before I submit it that he will be honest and constructive with me.
- ✓ Safety: I trust that if I share my struggles as a new manager with my peer she will respond with empathy and keep it confidential.
- ✓ Competency: I trust that if I ask Tom to present our group's report in my absence he will do a great job.
- ✓ Integrity: I trust that Rani will keep her word in the agreement we just made about her work.

How to Build Credibility and Trust
- ✓ Set a good example
- ✓ Keep commitments
- ✓ Tell the truth
- ✓ Be fair
- ✓ Don't have favorites
- ✓ Admit mistakes
- ✓ Be well-informed

✓ Understand the issues
✓ Share information
✓ Show respect

Building Respect
A mutual respect between individuals should underpin all working relationships. Demonstrating respect is fundamental to gaining trust and will form the foundations of a relationship in which ideas and opinions can be shared openly. Respect can be earned in a number of ways:
- ✓ Treat one another as equals. Even in relationships in which individuals have different levels of organizational seniority, colleagues should treat each other equally. 'Pulling rank' can make others in the relationship feel less valued.
- ✓ Share your knowledge with your colleagues. Offer them the benefit of your experience and encourage them to do the same.
- ✓ Recognize the achievements of others and make them aware that you value the contribution they make to your working relationship.
- ✓ Be honest. Committing to unrealistic time frames or making promises that can't be kept can be very damaging to working relationships. Be upfront with your colleague if you face constraints on time or resources, and suggest an alternative solution that is more achievable.

Understanding Others
Taking the time to understand your colleagues can be of real benefit to your working relationships. This means taking the time to learn what motivates and drives them to achieve their goals. Understanding can be developed in a number of ways, for example:
- ✓ Arranging an introductory meeting when you start working with someone for the first time to establish what you can expect from one another in the working relationship.
- ✓ Establishing shared objectives when embarking upon a new project or initiative to allow you to work towards a common goal.
- ✓ Using active listening skills during meetings and discussions. Active listening means listening intently to what someone is saying and making it clear to them throughout that you have heard and understood them.
- ✓ Finding out what each others' strengths are so you can agree on how best to share responsibilities when approaching tasks together.

Exercise
What areas would you need to work on to build your Credibility, especially keeping these 3 key Pillars of Trust, Respect and Understanding Others, in mind?
1.
2.
3.
4.
5.
6.
7.

Giving and Receiving Feedback

Feedback is likely to be more effective if:
- ✓ The person receiving it acknowledges the need for it; especially if the person requests for it
- ✓ It is timely; given near the time when the behavior has occurred
- ✓ It is skilful and professionally done
- ✓ If you consider the outcome to be developmental to both parties.
- ✓ You understand the motive behind it: Question your motive: If your motive is to show that you are better than the person or to put the person down, refrain from giving the feedback

What all can happen if you DO NOT provide suitable advice/ information or feedback on time?
- ✓ Misunderstanding
- ✓ Poor relationships/team working
- ✓ Wasted production
- ✓ Damage to machinery
- ✓ Unacceptable quality
- ✓ Waste of time and energies
- ✓ Customer complaints
- ✓ Drop in health, safety, security standards
- ✓ Credibility of organization affected
- ✓ Attrition (may lose even good people)

Exercise

What other areas or what else can happen if feedback is not provided on time?
1.
2.
3.
4.
5.

How to Skillfully Provide Feedback:
- ✓ Be descriptive, by providing information that describes the behavior and its impact on you; restrict the feedback to what you know e.g., behavior you have seen and how it has impacted you.
- ✓ It is about the giver of the feedback, not the person receiving the feedback. It is an exploration of the effect the person's behavior has had on you. (Note: the same behavior may not have that effect on others).
- ✓ Avoid exaggeration ("you always get this wrong"), labeling ("you are stupid"), and being judgmental
- ✓ Speak for yourself ("what I feel/experience when you ....") not for others ("Everyone gets upset when you ....")
- ✓ Don't press the person for any immediate response

✓ Face to face is the best-never by e-mail
✓ Observe the receiver's body language to assess the extent to which the feedback is being received.
✓ Adjust your feedback to ensure that the channels of communication remain open.

Exercise

What areas would you specifically need to work on to skillfully provide feedback?

1.
2.
3.
4.
5.

How to Skillfully Receive Feedback:

✓ Observe and listen actively to and when receiving feedback.
✓ Ask questions to clarify – "Could you give an example of that?", "When did that happen?", "Who else was there?
✓ If others where present during the behavior the feedback is about; ask them to offer feedback, what was the effect on them
✓ Acknowledge valid points
✓ Open yourself. Do not get defensive (you may feel it, don't act it).
✓ Stay focused on hearing what is being said.
✓ Take time to think about what has been said; if a response is necessary tell those offering the feedback that you will think about it and offer some response at a specified date/time.
✓ From feedback to negotiation of the relationship - "I would like ..."
What would you like the person to consider doing- "Because ..."
Why you believe it will help. "What do you think?"
Invite and hear the response; explore options

Exercise

What areas would you specifically need to work on to skillfully receive feedback?

1.
2.
3.
4.
5.

When Giving Feedback, Keep the following in Mind:

1. Do it often: Virtually no one thinks they get enough feedback and that is because virtually no one gives enough.

2. Do not be shy: Give feedback as close to the event it refers to as possible. This way, what happened is fresh in everybody's mind and it will be easier to learn from it.

3. Give it some meaning: Always provide the context before you give feedback. For example "I wanted to talk to you about the report that you wrote yesterday."

4. Be specific: Talk about what went well and what could have gone better for the individual or the team.
5. Describe actual behaviors where possible: Avoid the "sandwich effect" (good-bad-good) - it comes across as untruthful and dilutes the impact of good feedback.
6. Give a wider context: Describe the impact it had and on whom. This gives an idea of how important it is.
7. Be generous with positive feedback: With positive feedback describe what it tells you about the individual. Find a few positives that you can provide.
8. Allow people a chance to respond: If they would like time to reflect, let them, and agree to talk about it again at a future date. Do not force people to talk about it though.
9. Remain objective: Do not let your personal prejudices get the better of you. Remember you are giving feedback for the other person's benefit and not to vent your own spleen.
10. Build an action plan: With critical feedback make sure there is an agreed way to progress. Find the right time and place.

Handling External Working Relationships

In many organizations, developing relationships with people who do not work in the same location as you (e.g. colleagues based elsewhere, clients and suppliers) is a key aspect of working life. In these situations, face-to-face contact is often limited, or simply not possible, so it can take a little longer to build relationships. Suggestions for conducting successful relationships in this context are outlined below:

- ✓ Where possible, try to arrange at least one face-to-face meeting at the beginning of the relationship, to establish rapport.
- ✓ Without visual cues, it is easier to misunderstand someone when you are communicating by phone or email so ensure you maintain a straightforward communication style and avoid making comments, jokes or other uncalled for remarks that could be misinterpreted.
- ✓ Check understanding and any agreed actions at the end of phone calls. Make it clear in emails that you are available if further information is required.
- ✓ Maintain regular contact to keep the relationship on track. A short 'how are things?' email or a quick courtesy phone call can work wonders in helping to maintain a healthy working relationship.
- ✓ Always apply the same levels of professionalism as you would to internal relationships. Your conduct reflects your organization as well as you.

Managing Difficult and Challenging Relationships

Working in Toxic Places
Difficult people are part of every workplace you've ever known. Bad bosses can drive you crazy quickly and aggravating co-workers just add fuel to the fire. Most workers have found themselves saying "I really don't want to go to work tomorrow" at one point or another. But there's a fine line between wanting an extra day off and dreading going into work. Employees who dread work could be working in a toxic environment, which hurts productivity, employee wellbeing, customer relationships, and more.

Question to Ask when Dealing with Challenging Workplace Relationships
Here are a few questions to ask yourself (in no particular order) the next time you feel you are experiencing a difficult workplace relationship:
- ✓ Does it matter? Is this issue really worth your time and energy? If it isn't then don't get bogged down, just move on to your next priority. If it is, then it's worth the effort to resolve it properly.
- ✓ Why might it be happening? Everything has a cause. You may never know what that cause is, but if you assume that there is a good reason for the behavior then you stand a better chance of keeping your cool when you're feeling frustrated, annoyed, put-down, etc.
- ✓ Have you explained your position? Can you calmly and objectively tell them what they are doing and the impact it is having on you? They may not have realized the consequences of their actions.
- ✓ Have you asked about theirs? They may not want to tell you but at least you are giving them the opportunity.
- ✓ Have you clearly defined the problem? Is it really their lateness or does your annoyance stem from other issues?
- ✓ Is there any common ground? If you talk it through you may find you both want the same thing. Anything in common is a good starting point to resolving the conflict.
- ✓ Can you both have what you want? If you assume that you can and then try to find a way to make it happen you're more likely to be successful (in other words, think positive!)
- ✓ If not, where is the acceptable compromise? What could you both give up and still feel fairly treated?

How to respond to difficult people: Use these strategies for success.
1. Watch your attitude. When dealing with difficult people, the most important thing to remember is to have ultimate control of your attitude. You always have a choice as to how to respond to a given individual. You can get upset and frustrated, or you can remain calm and handle that person with tact.
2. Stay calm, cool, and collected. Losing your temper and flaring up at the other person typically isn't the best way to get him/her to collaborate with you. Try counting to 10, taking a break, walking away from the situation, having a cup of coffee or water or even

putting the person on the phone on hold for a short time. These techniques work because they break you away from the situation, giving you time to think what to do. Someone who is calm is seen as being in control, focused and more respectable. When the person you are dealing with sees that you are calm despite whatever he/she is doing, you will start getting their attention.

3. Understand the person's intentions. No one is difficult for the sake of being difficult. Even when it may seem that the person is just out to get you, there is always some underlying reason that is motivating them to act this way. Rarely is this motivation apparent. Try to identify the person's trigger: What is making him/her act in this manner? What is stopping him/her from cooperating with you? How can you help to meet his/her needs and resolve the situation?

4. Let the person know where you are coming from. One thing that can work is to let the person know your intentions behind what you are doing. Sometimes, they are being resistant because they think that you are just being difficult with them. Letting them in on the reason behind your actions and the full background of what is happening will enable them to empathize with your situation. This lets them get on-board much easier.

5. Use your brain and not your heart, but have heart. In other words, do not use emotions to handle a difficult person. When you use emotion, you are just reacting. Instead, use your mind to deal with the negative person or situation. When you do this, you are in control.

6. Weigh the situation and consequences. Evaluate the situation and think about the consequences of your actions. See beyond the immediate. Anticipate what could happen and whether you can live with that. Then act in a positive, confident manner.

7. Attack the issue, not the person. It never does any good to attack people. Obviously something happened that caused the conflict. Get to the issue and focus on it rather than on the person.

8. Listen. Listen carefully in order to understand the other person's point of view. Block out your own thoughts, judgments, and priorities and listen to the other person's concerns and feelings. Be a dispassionate observer, by remaining detached, neutral, and above the emotion of the conflict. Observe, listen, and let the other person know he's been heard, but do not allow yourself to come down into the scene. You did not make the person difficult, and you cannot "fix" them. You can, however, limit their influence, and not reinforce difficult behavior.

9. Define the problem. Are you clear on the real issue of conflict or is it just your perception? Ongoing communication helps clarify each person's perception of the situation, ensuring that the problem is clearly defined.

10. Use facts only. Stick to the facts when confronting someone. You will get more positive results when you deal with the facts than with the emotions around them.

11. Focus on what can be worked upon or put to action. Whatever it is, acknowledge that the situation has already occurred. Rather than focus on what you cannot change, focus on the actionable steps you can take to forward yourself in the situation.

12. Maintain each other's self-esteem. It's harmful to belittle others, and this diminishes your professional image. When confronting colleagues, make sure you communicate in a way that allows them to save face. Treat the other person with respect. As the golden rule says, "Do unto others as you would have them do unto you."

13. Re-instill the human touch by connecting with your colleagues on a personal level. Go out with them for lunches or dinners. Get to know them as people, and not colleagues. Learn more about their hobbies, their family, and their lives. Foster strong connections. These will go a long way in your work.

14. Focus on Future Behavior: People aren't the problem; it's the behavior that is the problem. A person can only change future behavior. A conversation filled with a history of mistakes generates defensiveness and shuts down communication.

15. Limit your interactions. If you have already tried everything above and the person is still not being receptive, the best way might be to just ignore. If you haven't been able to form any kind of useful relationship with your colleague then try to avoid working closely with them. After all, you have already done all that you can within your means. Get on your daily tasks and interface with the person only where needed.

Exercise

From some of the suggestions provided above, what strategies would you specifically need to work on to deal and cope up with difficult people in a professional manner?

1.
2.
3.
4.
5.
6.
7.
8.

Addressing Differences and Diversity

It is inevitable that, at some point, you will encounter challenges in your working relationships. When a difficult situation occurs, it is important that it is addressed promptly. There are number of ways you can do this, for example:

- ✓ Have an open conversation with the person concerned. This may seem awkward at first, but failing to address problems can lead to more serious issues. Outline your concerns concisely, supporting your points with examples. Stress your commitment to the relationship and your wish to find a solution that works for both of you.
- ✓ Listen carefully to your colleague's point of view and take their comments on board. Clarify any actions you or your colleague might need to take to help the relationship get back on track.
- ✓ Avoid the temptation to badmouth your colleague or approach the issue with their manager, before you have discussed it with them personally. If you are unsure whether speaking to your colleague directly is the right thing to do, take the advice of someone you trust in the organization, such as another manager or director.

What you could do to Manage Diversity

- ✓ Accept that differences exist and are healthy
- ✓ Discover, Understand, Accept and Inventory the differences that exist among your team members
- ✓ Affirm the value of Team members differences
- ✓ Make a habit to build others self-worth/ self-esteem
- ✓ Don't let Ego come between
- ✓ Make a habit to listen to others for better understanding
- ✓ Try looking at their views and perspectives with an open mind
- ✓ Keep asking: What are their positive traits that the team can benefit from

Dealing with Criticism

How to Deliver Criticism the Proper Way
- ✓ Choose the time and place carefully: Find a private place where you know you won't be interrupted that is convenient to both
- ✓ Listen impartially: Not showing any negative or defensive emotions when listening will stop you appearing vulnerable or fragile.
- ✓ Summarize what the other person has said: This means you have understood them correctly and also that you have taken it all in.
- ✓ Ask questions: The more specific the criticism the more helpful. Find out what you did and when that gave them their impression. This will mean you will not make the same mistake again.
- ✓ Be as specific as you can. Ideally, with examples. Do not generalize
- ✓ Avoid general and negative 'triggers.': Words and phrases that will put the employee on the defensive, such as "you always" and "you never."
- ✓ Criticism is rarely groundless but often exaggerated: Decide which elements are useful and what you can do differently to be more effective from now on.
- ✓ Focus on the future. Once you have covered the details, move on to the future immediately, on what changes you would like to see.
- ✓ Think about how the person who criticizes you looks at the world: Could they have been trying to help? Are they under pressure themselves? Think about why they have these views about you. This could open up to some useful self awareness.
- ✓ Ask those who criticize you for their advice: By making them part of the solution, they are less likely to criticize you in the future.
- ✓ Thank people who criticize you: Not only have they given you free information but you have now also disarmed them.
- ✓ Reframe criticism which focuses on what went badly: Consider what positive steps you can take to improve in the future and what you have learnt from not succeeding.
- ✓ If you are angry, take it out on something, not someone: It is understandable to be annoyed but not very useful.
- ✓ Praise others for what they are doing well: It will give you the moral high ground and make you popular (as well as reinforcing productive behavior).

Exercise

What steps would you follow in dealing with criticism? Outline

1.
2.
3.
4.
5.
6.
7.
8.

Keeping Discussions from Turning into Arguments

The only way you can make sure you never lose an argument, to paraphrase Dale Carnegie, is to avoid getting into one in the first place.

Tips to keep discussions from Turning into Arguments:
1. Do not argue: Refuse to get drawn into an argument. Respect the other person as much as you honor your own values. Be assertive without resorting to aggression.
2. Seek areas of agreement: Often we agree with people in principle but disagree with them in practice (we want the same thing but have different ideas of how to accomplish it). Find those areas of agreement. Make them clear. Try always to make the other person a fellow problem-solver, neither an opponent nor a friend.
3. Focus on interests, not positions: An issue is what we want or need. A position is a way of achieving it. Avoid getting attached to your positions so that you do not lose sight of your interests. It is often easier to negotiate and compromise around interests than around positions.
4. Try to see things from the other person's point-of-view: There is a reason why other people act and think the way they do - however illogical, wrong-headed, or misguided as it may seem to you. If you criticize them or show disapproval for their reasoning, they will only harden in their resolution. They will resent and resist you. Seek, instead, to discover their hidden reasons, and you will find the key to their motivation.
 5. Ask clarifying questions: Ask open-ended questions. As noted earlier under the chapter of 'Questioning and Listening', closed questions-like "Do you agree with my proposal?" –these limit people's ability to express themselves. Open-ended questions – like "How do you feel about my proposal?" will give them freedom and give you more information.
 6. Listen: Spend more time listening than speaking (you cannot get yourself into trouble by listening, but you sure can start an argument by speaking). Listen with your body, your eyes and your mind as well as with your ears. Try to understand what people mean, without getting caught up in the exact words they say. Make them feel understood, and they will be much more likely to try to understand you.
7. If you are wrong, admit it: There is nothing wrong with changing your opinion, once you have gained new information or perspective. As a matter of fact, it is the sign of wisdom and maturity. Remember that you have been wrong in the past even when you thought you were right, and admit that you might be wrong this time.
8. If you are right, allow the other person to save face: You are trying to win people's cooperation, not to prove them wrong. Your kindness will do more to gain their goodwill than anything else. Do not let ego come in between

Exercise
What steps would you take to prevent Discussions from turning to Arguments?
1.
2.
3.
4.

5.
6.
7.
8.

Resolving and Managing Conflicts

Conflict is a normal, and even healthy, part of relationships. After all, two people can't
be expected to agree on everything at all times. Since relationship conflicts
are inevitable, learning to deal with them in a healthy way is crucial. When conflict is
mismanaged, it can harm the relationship and hamper progress. But when handled in
a respectful and positive way, conflict provides an opportunity for growth, ultimately
strengthening the bond between two people and can keep your personal
and professional relationships strong and growing.

Successful conflict resolution depends on your ability to:
- ✓ Keep the bigger picture in mind while focusing on the future.
- ✓ Manage stress while remaining alert and calm. By staying calm, you can
  accurately read and interpret verbal and nonverbal communication.
- ✓ Control your emotions and behavior. When you're in control of your emotions,
  you can communicate your needs without threatening, frightening, or
  punishing others.
- ✓ Pay attention to the feelings being expressed as well as the spoken words of
  others.
- ✓ Be aware of and respectful of differences. By avoiding disrespectful words
  and actions,

Healthy and unhealthy ways of managing and resolving conflict
Conflict triggers strong emotions and can lead to hurt feelings, disappointment,
and discomfort. When handled in an unhealthy manner, it can cause irreparable rifts,
resentments, and breakups. But when conflict is resolved in a healthy way, it increases
our understanding of one another, builds trust, and strengthens our relationship bonds.
Unhealthy responses to conflict are characterized by:
- ✓ An inability to recognize and respond to matters of great importance to
  the other person
- ✓ Abusive, explosive, angry, hurtful, and resentful reactions
- ✓ The withdrawal of love, resulting in rejection, isolation, shaming, and fear of
  abandonment
- ✓ The expectation of bad outcomes
- ✓ The fear and avoidance of conflict

Healthy responses to conflict are characterized by:
- ✓ The capacity to recognize and respond to important matters
- ✓ A readiness to forgive and forget
- ✓ The ability to seek compromise and avoid punishing
- ✓ A belief that resolution can support the interests and needs of both parties

Steps in Resolving Conflicts
1. Acknowledge that conflict exists
2. Agree on a mutually acceptable time and place to discuss the conflict.
3. State the problem as you see it and list your concerns.

4. Identify the "real" conflict
5. Withhold judgments, accusations, and generalized statements ("always" or "never").
6. Let the other person have his/her say. Hear all points of view. Do not interrupt or contradict.
7. Do not allow name-calling, put-downs, threats, obscenities, yelling or intimidating behavior.
8. Listen and ask questions. Ask fact-based open questions (who? where? what? when? how?. See more on Question techniques under the respective chapter) to make sure you understand the situation. Ask exploratory questions (what if? what are you saying? is this the only solution to your problem? what if did such and such? are there other alternatives to this situation?). Avoid accusatory "why" questions (why are you like that?).
9. Reconfirm/ Paraphrase. Use your own words to restate what you think the other person means and wants. Acknowledge person's feelings and perceptions.
10. Stick to one conflict at a time- the issue at hand. Do not change the subject or allow it to be changed. ("I understand your concern but I'd like to finish what we're talking about at the moment before we discuss it.")
11. Focus on Present NOT past: Don't hold on to hurts- focus on what you can do to solve the problem
12. Seek common ground. What do you agree on? What are your shared concerns? Together explore ways to resolve the conflict
13. Brainstorm solutions to the conflict that allow everyone to win.
14. Request behavior changes only. Do not ask others to change their attitudes. Do not ask them to "feel" differently about something. Do not ask them to "be" different. If you want them to "stop doing" something, suggest an alternative solution.
15. Agree to the best way to resolve the conflict
16. Set a timetable for implementing it. Who will do what by when?
17. Gain agreement on, and responsibility for, a solution
18. Schedule a follow-up session to review the resolution
19. If the discussion breaks down, reschedule another time to meet. Consider bringing in a third party.
20. Work on building back your relationship

Guidelines to keep in mind when fire-fighting
Managing and Resolving Conflicts requires: Emotional Maturity, Self-control and Empathy. Here are some points to keep in mind:
- ✓ Make the Relationship your Priority: Don't look at 'winning' an argument- Be respectful of others view point
- ✓ Remain calm. Try not to overreact to difficult situations. By remaining calm it will be more likely that others will consider your viewpoint.
- ✓ Express feelings in words, not actions. Telling someone directly and honestly how you feel can be a very powerful form of communication. If you start to feel so angry or upset that you feel you may lose control, take "time out" and do something to help yourself feel better.
- ✓ Be specific about what is bothering you. Vague complaints are hard to work on.

- ✓ Pick your Battles: Consider-is this issue really worth the time/ energy. Eg; parking space- not wanting to surrender after circling 15 minutes…but if enough space around is it worth it arguing!
- ✓ Deal with only one issue at a time. Don't introduce other topics until each is fully discussed. This avoids the "kitchen sink" effect where people throw in all their complaints while not allowing anything to be resolved.
- ✓ No "hitting below the belt." Attacking areas of personal sensitivity creates an atmosphere of distrust, anger, and vulnerability.
- ✓ Avoid accusations. Accusations will cause others to defend themselves. Instead, talk about how someone's actions made you feel
- ✓ Don't generalize. Avoid words like "never" or "always." Such generalizations are usually inaccurate and will heighten tensions.
- ✓ Don't stockpile. Storing up lots of grievances and hurt feelings over time is counterproductive. It's almost impossible to deal with numerous old problems for which interpretations may differ. Try to deal with problems as they arise.
- ✓ Avoid clamming up. When one person becomes silent and stops responding to the other, frustration and anger can result. Positive results can only be attained with two-way communication
- ✓ Be willing to Forgive
- ✓ Know when to let something go: If a conflict is getting nowhere, you can choose to disengage and move on!

Exercise

What would your Strategies be to handle Conflicts more professionally? List

1.
2.
3.
4.
5.
6.
7.
8.
9.
10.

How to Win People's Cooperation

1. Make people feel understood: Spend less time trying to make people understand what you want, and more time making them feel understood.

2. Find common ground: Show people how their needs, values and dreams mesh with yours. To do so, you have to understand their values and concerns. See things from their point of view. Be sympathetic with their feelings. Then show them how cooperating with you can help them achieve what they want.

3. Listen: Listening is the best way to make people feel understood and at the same time to find common ground. Ask open-ended questions, the kinds that invite people's careful consideration and honesty. Try to understand what people mean, without getting hung up on the literal meaning of their words. And acknowledge their thoughts and feelings (which is not the same thing as agreeing with them).

4. Do not argue: The person you defeat in an argument today may be the person whose cooperation you may need tomorrow. And the more you try to prove them wrong, the harder they will resist you. People may feel overwhelmed and stop arguing with you. But that does not mean you have won them over. Remember, most of the time, when you win an argument, you lose an ally.

5. Care about the people you want to influence: If you are concerned about the people you are trying to win over, if you value their needs and dreams, they will know it and they will reciprocate. They will communicate more freely, speaking their mind more openly and listening more attentively. They will give you the benefit of the doubt and they will want to cooperate.

6. Be open for other's ideas: Do not try to impose your ideas or thoughts on others. Listen to and value the ideas of the people that work for you or with whom you work together. Be open-minded and feel confident with sharing the ideas with others. Even, request for new ideas to gain people's support and cooperation.

7. Help people believe the change is possible: People often know, although they will not often admit, that they need to change. They feel a vague uneasiness, sensing that things will not work out the way they want. But they persist in doing what they have always done, thinking they are doing the best they can. Show them a better way, but more importantly convince them that the change is possible. Do not just give them a solution but offer them confidence.

8. Time your request well: There is a time and season for everything, especially for asking for support. When people are feeling stressed out, anxious, angry, resentful or threatened, they are not really receptive. Do what you can to reassure them and to make them feel safe and you increase your chances of winning their support. Look for "moments of influence", times when they feel capable and confident, and make your best case then.

Keys for Building Strong Relationships

Finally, what can you do to build Healthy and Strong Work Relationships? Here are some thoughts that can help you?

- ✓ Work on developing your people skills: Good relationships start with good people skills. In other words, how well you collaborate, communicate, commit and deal with conflict.
- ✓ Identify relationship needs: Look at the relationship needs of others as well as yourself. Do you know what they need from you? And do you know what you need from others? Understanding these needs can be instrumental in building better relationships
- ✓ Establish a set of values or 'ground rules' for yourself and apply them to every working relationship you develop: Adopt a consistent approach and aim to achieve the same degree of trust, respect and understanding with every person you work with.
- ✓ Respect Others: Respect others and their opinions. Never make others feel neglected, and not being harsh on their face when you disagree with them. Respect their inputs and try to explain your point of view with a little more empathy.
- ✓ Speak positively about the people you work with especially to your boss: Always speak positively to others and provide quality feedback about the people you work with. Shared information- positive or negative often comes back to the person being discussed. That will build trust.
- ✓ Listen Actively: Practice active listening when you talk to your customers and colleagues. People respond to those who truly listen to what they have to say. Focus on listening more than you talk, and you'll quickly become known as someone who can be trusted.
- ✓ Set time aside to build relationships: Set a portion of your day towards relationship building, even if it's just a few minutes. Strengthen your relationships by aiming to get to know your colleagues better outside the workplace. Attend social events and group activities when you have the opportunity, to build rapport and spend time with your colleagues in a more relaxed setting. These little interactions help build the foundation of a good relationship, especially if they're face-to-face.

- ✓ Ask the people with whom you work most closely to provide you with some feedback on your working relationship and to highlight anything they might like you to do differently: Agree on steps you can both take to improve the relationship, if necessary.
- ✓ Learn to appreciate others: Show your appreciation whenever someone helps you. Everyone wants to feel that their work is appreciated. So, genuinely compliment the people around you when they do something well. This will open the door to great work relationships.
- ✓ Write thank-you notes: Write notes of appreciation to the people who are doing exemplary work, making positive contributions, and going above the call of duty. Everyone likes to be appreciated and will feel closer to you
- ✓ Be Positive: Focus on being positive. Positivity is attractive and contagious, and it will help strengthen your relationships with your colleagues. No one wants to be around someone who's negative all the time.
- ✓ Be proactive and help wherever you can without being asked: Where possible, offer your knowledge and experience to colleagues and find a way to help with work your colleagues are undertaking. Ask how you can get involved. This will form a closer connection because you are working directly with others to help them meet their goals. They will appreciate your support and get to know you better, which is vital to creating a more connected working relationship.
- ✓ Manage your boundaries: Make sure that you set and manage boundaries properly – all of us want to have friends at work, but, occasionally, a friendship can start to impact our jobs, especially when a friend or colleague begins to monopolize our time. If this happens, it's important that you're assertive about your boundaries, and that you know how much time you can devote during the work day for social interactions.
- ✓ Always keep your commitment and deliver as promised: Nothing is worse than someone who fails to deliver on a promise or consistently misses deadlines. There is no quicker way to spoil your reputation and damage potential working relationships than failing to follow through on work
- ✓ Never gossip: Totally avoid gossip. Office politics and "gossip" are major relationship killers at work. If you're experiencing conflict with someone in your group, talk to them directly about the problem. Gossiping about the situation with other colleagues will only worsen the situation, and will cause mistrust and animosity between you.
- ✓ Identify someone within your professional network who has strong relationship-building skills (like a mentor) and ask them to coach or advise you on how you can improve your own approach to developing relationships.

Exercise

What more would you like to add to the above points to build on Healthy and Strong Relationships?

Conclusion

In conclusion, let us remind ourselves that:
Life requires us to effectively manage 4 Key components if we have to be successful....Think of the acronym **C.R.A.F.T:**
Change
Relationships
Attitude
Finances
Time
Anyone of these 5 components if not managed well, can lead to a disrupted life, and as we can see 'Relationships' is one of the essential keys
Relationship building skills are therefore crucial in business, helping create the foundation of care, trust and connection we need to grow. They enable us to get the best from teams and collaborators, and work towards your goals. Whether you are working with someone who sits next to you or someone who works on the other side of the world, building relationships is most essential to achieving your objectives and those of the organization. A successful relationship is built on trust, respect and understanding, and requires ongoing investment from both parties. When difficulties arise in the relationship, they should be addressed openly and in a professional manner to ensure the relationship continues to develop
Inevitably differences of opinion will arise between leaders, managers, colleagues and external partners. But, good relationship building skills will help stop conflicts from escalating, and refocus on a better path. When problems do arise, these tools will see you through a crisis.
Building good work relationships can take hard work. It requires time, patience, and self-awareness. But putting in the emotional labor and building good work relationships will help you feel more connected to your colleagues and increase your overall job satisfaction. Healthy and positive work relationships will make your job less stressful and enjoyable. It will cut out the mundane factor that often plagues an employee in the long run. In fact businesses are increasingly looking for candidates with strong relationship skills. A company culture that encourages employees to maintain healthy relationships can go a long way towards enhancing employee well-being.

Exercise
Try completing the Exercises below to help in Building Healthy Relationships within your Team:

1. What are some ways to create trust and bonding on my team?

2. How can you promote healthy conflict?

3. What are some ways to create commitment into each team member?

4. How can you instill accountability in your team?

About the Author
'GERARD ASSEY'

Gerard Assey is a Graduate in Economics, a PGD in Management (HRD) and holds a Doctorate in Leadership. Gerard holds several International Qualifications in Sales, Debt Collection, Training & Teaching, and is a 'Fellow' of the prestigious 'Institute of Sales & Marketing Management'-UK, a Certified NLP Practitioner, a 'Certified Trainer', an 'Accredited Management Teacher-Behavioural Sciences', a 'Certified Competency Facilitator', a 'Certified Management Consultant'- (the International credentials of a professional management consultant, awarded in accordance with global standards of the ICMCI); and a Certification from the University of Michigan in 'Successful Negotiation: Essential Strategies and Skills'

He is also a Member of the 'National Association of Sales Professionals' backed with several years experience in varied industries, both in India and Overseas. He also holds an 'Etiquette Consultant' Certification from the USA (by Sue Fox, Author of Best Seller: 'Business Etiquette for Dummies'. She has trained some of the top celebrities' world over). He was also a recipient of a scholarship for extensive training in Japan on 'Corporate Management for India'.

Gerard Assey is 'Founder & Chief Corporate Trainer' of the Group: '**Citius, Altius, Fortius Unlimited'**- an organization that **celebrated 20 years of Glorious Service** in 2021, focusing on 3 Core Competencies: **People. Performance. Profit**; in functional areas of Sales & Marketing, HR & Organizational Development, covering Recruitment, Training & Consultancy!

Having managed organizations with large Sales Forces in India & Overseas, his specialization cover extensive areas of Sales Training (All levels - Presentation, Negotiation, Key/ Strategic Accounts Management & Managerial Skills for all sectors), Bid Proposal/ Capture Planning/ Management Trainings, Retail Sales, Customer Service & Customer Retention Programs, Training for Prevention & Collection of Debt, Self & Personal Development Programs (Time Management, Teamwork & Team Building, Business Etiquette & Personal Grooming, Leadership & Managerial Skills, People Management Skills, Train-the-Trainer etc), including preparation of Custom-designed Business Manuals for Internal (HR, Induction, and Sales etc) & External use (Instruction, User Manuals).

Gerard has successfully conducted over 5900 Trainings & Workshops (as of July 2022) all across India, Middle East, Africa, Europe & S.E. Asia. Besides public programs conducted regularly, both in India & Overseas, he has some of the top names as clients whom he services from Single Owners to large Public & Government undertakings, covering all sectors, for their in-house needs.

His website: www.CollectionSkills.com is the only one in this part of the world to be featured in the 'Collections & Credit Risk Magazine-USA' under 'Who's Who in Training' and <u>ranks TOP</u>, along with other websites listed below on most search engines.

Gerard is author of 42 books already (as on Aug 2022),
A few of the business related books being:
1. Bite-sized Bits on Commonsense Management
2. Heart to Heart on Life's Principles'
3. How to become a Successful Manager
4. The Sales Professionals' Master Workbook of S.Y.S.T.E.M.S
5. The Professional Business Email Etiquette Handbook & Guide
6. The Professional Business Video-Conferencing Etiquette Handbook & Guide
7. Professional Presentation Skills
8. Exceptional Customer Service
9. Professional Tele-Marketing Skills
10. Professional Debt Collection Skills
11. The G.R.E.A.T. Sales & Service Workbook
12. Sales Training Advantage for Results (*The Ultimate Sales Training Manual to enable you stand out as a S.T.A.R.*)
13. CEO Daily Planner & Organizer
14. The Sales Professionals' Master Daily Planner
15. The Professional Debt Collector's Master Daily Planner
16. My Daily Planner & Organizer
17. MY EMERGENCY INFORMATION RECORD (Family Emergency & Peace of Mind Planner)
18. The Ultimate Therapist & Counselors Planner and Organizer
19. Building an Ethical Workplace

Besides regularly contributing to business & trade journals, including international ones such as the 'Creative Training Techniques' and the 'Sales News' of the U.S.A, He is also a member of several prestigious bodies & trade associations, having participated in many Conferences & Workshops in India & Overseas.
Prior to his last assignment of leading & managing a large MNC as head, Gerard had a 3-year stint in the Middle East as a Consultant with a leading British Consultancy Firm.

As the past 'Official Country Representative' for the International Business Award- 'THE STEVIES'-(the business world's own Oscar) for about 4 years- he ensured a few Indian companies that qualify for the same every year!

Gerard can be contacted at:
E: mail: <u>training@Sales-Training.in</u>
<u>training@CollectionSkills.com</u>
Websites:
<u>www.Sales-Training.in</u>
<u>www.EtiquetteWorks.in</u>
<u>www.CollectionSkills.com</u>
<u>www.RetailSalesTraining.in</u>
<u>www.SalesTrainingIndia.com</u>
<u>www.ManualPreparation.com</u>
<u>www.TrainingWithPuppets.com</u>
<u>www.FirstContactAcademy.com</u>
<u>www.SalesAndMarketingRecruiter.com</u>

Our TRAININGS & BOOKS that can help your team

- ✓ **Sales Effectiveness**: Selling Skills for any Sector: Service/ Logistics/ FMCG Realty/ Insurance & Finance/ Media/ SPA's, Health Clubs & Salons/ Key Account Management, Effective Negotiation Skills/ Bid & Proposal Management Skills/ Retail Sales Training: Any Sector (Auto, Jewelry, Clothing, Luxury etc)
- ✓ **Customer Service Skills**-Complaints Handling & Customer Retention
- ✓ **Debt Prevention & Collection Skills**
- ✓ **Etiquette & Grooming**
- ✓ **Leadership & Managerial Skills**
- ✓ **Self & Personal Development Skills**: Presentation Skills/ Effective Communication Skills/Business Proposal Writing Skills/ Problem Solving & Decision Making Skills/ Empowering Secretaries-The perfect PA! (For Secretaries & PA's)/ Effective Time Management/ Teamwork & Teambuilding/ P.R.I.D.E- **P**ersonal **R**esponsibility **I**n **D**elivering **E**xcellence